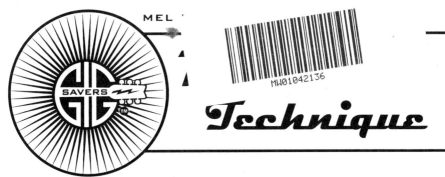

MEL

SAVERS

Technique

FOR SERIOUS PLAYERS

by COREY CHRISTIANSEN

1 2 3 4 5 6 7 8 9 0

Killer Technique

The **Gig Savers**™ series has been designed to give aspiring guitarists answers to common questions in a brief, affordable, yet informative fashion. *Killer Technique* provides concepts and daily routines to help players get more control over their instrument by improving their technique and avoiding injury.

Having good, efficient technique is paramount in becoming a great guitarist. By improving technique, a guitarist can do more by working less. Many of the exercises in this book are very basic and may seem simple at first, but get harder. Even the easiest exercises, played perfectly, can be challenging for an experienced guitarist. The idea is to take these workouts slowly. By doing so, proper technique will be acquired and hand injury will be avoided.

It is a constant battle to synchronize the right and left hand. If it was easy, everybody would be able to play the guitar on a high level. Many guitarists have found success in building technique by working the right and left hand separately. If a new technique is being worked on to develop the right hand, make the exercise easy for the left in the beginning. If a technique is being worked on for left-hand development, make it relatively easy for the right hand. As the level of technique for both the right and left hand increases, what used to be hard will become easy for both hands. Before long, concepts that were previously hard for the right hand will be easy material used to supplement an exercise that is difficult for the left hand. It will be apparent which hand is being worked in each of the exercises. Hopefully, each guitarist will use these ideas as a springboard to create workouts of their own. Constructing workouts can be a never-ending project. The trick is to find a methodical way to create and stay organized.

The exercises in this book are not written in standard notation or tab. The patterns that make up the exercises are written with string numbers, fret numbers and/or a fretboard diagram. This will allow guitarists, regardless of reading abilities, of all styles and all levels, to use the exercises.

Left–Hand Workout

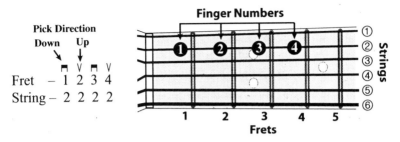

Finger Numbers

Pick Direction
Down   Up

Fret – 1 2 3 4
String – 2 2 2 2

Frets

Strings

The first exercises are for the left hand. Starting in the first fret, slowly play the following pattern up and down all six strings. DO NOT change the direction of the pattern when the string order is reversed. (That will come later, just play 1-2-3-4.) Only use down-strokes. Every exercise in this book should be played slowly and perfectly before playing them fast. Each note should get the same amount of time. This means that the rhythm for each note is equal and should be steady. If practicing with a metronome, each note can get a beat, a half a beat, or a quarter of a beat. When alternate picking is introduced, eighth (half a beat) and sixteenth (quarter of a beat) notes should be used when practicing with a metronome. The goal is to be able to rip through the exercise flawlessly, but accurate speed will not come without mastering these exercises at a relatively slow speed at first.

* Fret:	1-2-3-4	1-2-3-4	1-2-3-4	1-2-3-4	1-2-3-4	1-2-3-4
String:	1-1-1-1	2-2-2-2	3-3-3-3	4-4-4-4	5-5-5-5	6-6-6-6

Reverse String Order

Fret:	1-2-3-4	1-2-3-4	1-2-3-4	1-2-3-4	1-2-3-4	1-2-3-4
String:	6-6-6-6	5-5-5-5	4-4-4-4	3-3-3-3	2-2-2-2	1-1-1-1

* Because this exercise is shown in first position, the fret number also corresponds to the left-hand finger number.

This exercise is a moveable pattern. It can be moved into any fret or position. Try moving the pattern up one fret each time it is played through all six strings.

Now apply alternate picking (down- and up-strokes) to the same fingering pattern. To begin, play each note more than once. Pick each note two or four times for each pattern. This will help the right hand become synchronized with the left hand. When a reasonable comfort level is achieved, move to alternate picking attacking each note once.

	⊓ V ⊓ V	⊓ V ⊓ V	⊓ V ⊓ V	⊓ V ⊓ V	
Fret:	1-1-1-1	2-2-2-2	3-3-3-3	4-4-4-4	Repeat Down and
String:	1-1-1-1	1-1-1-1	1-1-1-1	1-1-1-1	Up All Six Strings

	⊓ V	⊓ V	⊓ V	⊓ V	
Fret:	1-1	2-2	3-3	4-4	Repeat Down and
String:	1-1	1-1	1-1	1-1	Up All Six Strings

	⊓ V ⊓ V	
Fret:	1-2-3-4	Repeat Down and
String:	1-1-1-1	Up All Six Strings

If a pause or unclear note is heard, isolate the two fingers that are not linking up and practice them separately. For example, many people have a difficult time playing smoothly between the third and fourth finger. For this case a smaller, more isolated pattern can be used throughout all six strings to strengthen that finger combination. This is a good practice for any weak finger combinations. Isolate and master.

	3-4	3-4	3-4	3-4	
Fret:	3-4	3-4	3-4	3-4	Repeat Down and
String:	1-1	1-1	1-1	1-1	Up All Six Strings

All of the permutations of 1-2-3-4 are given on the following page. It is a good idea to pick one or two ses to master at a time. It is better to master a few of them than to play all of them mediocre.

1-2-3-4	2-1-3-4	3-1-2-4	4-1-2-3
1-2-4-3	2-1-4-3	3-1-4-2	4-1-3-2
1-3-2-4	2-3-1-4	3-2-1-4	4-2-1-3
1-3-4-2	2-3-4-1	3-2-4-1	4-2-3-1
1-4-2-3	2-4-1-3	3-4-1-2	4-3-1-2
1-4-3-2	2-4-3-1	3-4-2-1	4-3-2-1

Once smooth alternate picking is achieved, use any of the following left-hand patterns. Remember to keep the pattern the same while playing on all six strings down and up. DO NOT reverse the order. It is a good idea to work with a pattern until it is comfortable. Also, each of these patterns are moveable. A typical workout could follow this type of pattern.

Using pattern 1-2-3-4 (any pattern can be used), repeat through strings 1-6. Then move up a fret and continue with strings 6-1. Reverse the direction when the fourth finger reaches the twelfth fret. This is a great warm-up exercise as well as a technique building exercise.

Strings 1–6. Pattern: 1-2-3-4 (any pattern can be used)

Pos. I

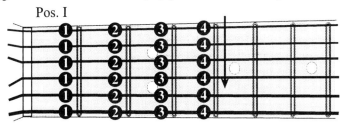

Strings 6–1

Pos. II

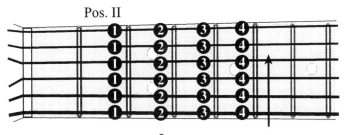

Strings 1–6, etc. Reverse when the 4th finger reaches the twelfth fret.

Pos. III

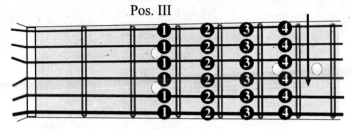

Right-Hand Workout

"Cross-picking" is alternate picking two notes on different strings. Alternate picking on one string is fairly easy compared to cross-picking. The following exercises will help develop alternate picking and cross picking. All of the exercises adhere to strict alternate picking and should be played slowly at first.

The following exercises use only open strings in the beginning. As with the other exercises, play the patterns from the sixth string to the first string and then reverse the direction.

①

Fret:	0-0-0-0	0-0-0-0	0-0-0-0	0-0-0-0	0-0-0-0	0-0-0-0
String:	2-1-2-1	2-1-2-1	3-2-3-2	3-2-3-2	4-3-4-3	4-3-4-3

Fret:	0-0-0-0	0-0-0-0	0-0-0-0	0-0-0-0
String:	5-4-5-4	5-4-5-4	6-5-6-5	6-5-6-5

②

Fret:	0-0-0-0	0-0-0-0	0-0-0-0	0-0-0-0	0-0-0-0
String:	2-1-2-1	3-2-3-2	4-3-4-3	5-4-5-4	6-5-6-5

③

Fret:	0-0	0-0	0-0	0-0	0-0
String:	2-1	3-2	4-3	5-4	6-5

⑮

	⊓ V ⊓ V
Fret:	0-0-0-0
String:	1-6-1-6

⑯

	⊓ V ⊓ V
Fret:	0-0-0-0
String:	6-1-6-1

⑰

	⊓ V ⊓ V	⊓ V ⊓ V	⊓ V ⊓ V	⊓ V ⊓ V	⊓ V ⊓ V	⊓ V ⊓ V
Fret:	0-0-0-0	0-0-0-0	0-0-0-0	0-0-0-0	0-0-0-0	0-0-0-0
String:	2-1-1-2	2-1-1-2	3-2-2-3	3-2-2-3	4-3-3-4	4-3-3-4

	⊓ V ⊓ V	⊓ V ⊓ V	⊓ V ⊓ V	⊓ V ⊓ V
Fret:	0-0-0-0	0-0-0-0	0-0-0-0	0-0-0-0
String:	5-4-4-5	5-4-4-5	6-5-5-6	6-5-5-6

⑱

	⊓ V ⊓ V	⊓ V ⊓ V	⊓ V ⊓ V	⊓ V ⊓ V	⊓ V ⊓ V
Fret:	0-0-0-0	0-0-0-0	0-0-0-0	0-0-0-0	0-0-0-0
String:	2-1-1-2	3-2-2-3	4-3-3-4	5-4-4-5	6-5-5-6

⑲

	⊓ V ⊓ V	⊓ V ⊓ V	⊓ V ⊓ V	⊓ V ⊓ V	⊓ V ⊓ V	⊓ V ⊓ V
Fret:	0-0-0-0	0-0-0-0	0-0-0-0	0-0-0-0	0-0-0-0	0-0-0-0
String:	1-2-2-1	1-2-2-1	2-3-3-2	2-3-3-2	3-4-4-3	3-4-4-3

	⊓ V ⊓ V	⊓ V ⊓ V	⊓ V ⊓ V	⊓ V ⊓ V
Fret:	0-0-0-0	0-0-0-0	0-0-0-0	0-0-0-0
String:	4-5-5-4	4-5-5-4	5-6-6-5	5-6-6-5

⑳

	⊓ V ⊓ V	⊓ V ⊓ V	⊓ V ⊓ V	⊓ V ⊓ V	⊓ V ⊓ V
Fret:	0-0-0-0	0-0-0-0	0-0-0-0	0-0-0-0	0-0-0-0
String:	1-2-2-1	2-3-3-2	3-4-4-3	4-5-5-4	5-6-6-5

㉑

	⊓ V ⊓ V	⊓ V ⊓ V	⊓ V ⊓ V	⊓ V ⊓ V
Fret:	0-0-0-0	0-0-0-0	0-0-0-0	0-0-0-0
String:	3-1-1-3	3-1-1-3	4-2-2-4	4-2-2-4

	⊓ V ⊓ V	⊓ V ⊓ V	⊓ V ⊓ V	⊓ V ⊓ V
Fret:	0-0-0-0	0-0-0-0	0-0-0-0	0-0-0-0
String:	5-3-3-5	5-3-3-5	6-4-4-6	6-4-4-6

㉒

	⊓ V ⊓ V	⊓ V ⊓ V	⊓ V ⊓ V	⊓ V ⊓ V
Fret:	0-0-0-0	0-0-0-0	0-0-0-0	0-0-0-0
String:	3-1-1-3	4-2-2-4	5-3-3-5	6-4-4-6

	⊓ V ⊓ V	⊓ V ⊓ V	⊓ V ⊓ V	⊓ V ⊓ V
Fret:	0-0-0-0	0-0-0-0	0-0-0-0	0-0-0-0
String:	1-3-3-1	2-4-4-2	3-5-5-3	4-6-6-4

㉓

	⊓ V ⊓ V	⊓ V ⊓ V	⊓ V ⊓ V	⊓ V ⊓ V
Fret:	0-0-0-0	0-0-0-0	0-0-0-0	0-0-0-0
String:	1-3-3-1	1-3-3-1	2-4-4-2	2-4-4-2

	⊓ V ⊓ V	⊓ V ⊓ V	⊓ V ⊓ V	⊓ V ⊓ V
Fret:	0-0-0-0	0-0-0-0	0-0-0-0	0-0-0-0
String:	3-5-5-3	3-5-5-3	4-6-6-4	4-6-6-4

㉔

	⊓ V ⊓ V	⊓ V ⊓ V	⊓ V ⊓ V	⊓ V ⊓ V	⊓ V ⊓ V	⊓ V ⊓ V
Fret:	0-0-0-0	0-0-0-0	0-0-0-0	0-0-0-0	0-0-0-0	0-0-0-0
String:	4-1-1-4	4-1-1-4	5-2-2-5	5-2-2-5	6-3-3-6	6-3-3-6

㉕

	⊓ V ⊓ V	⊓ V ⊓ V	⊓ V ⊓ V
Fret:	0-0-0-0	0-0-0-0	0-0-0-0
String:	4-1-1-4	5-2-2-5	6-3-3-6

10

26

	⊓ V ⊓ V	⊓ V ⊓ V	⊓ V ⊓ V	⊓ V ⊓ V	⊓ V ⊓ V	⊓ V ⊓ V
Fret:	0-0-0-0	0-0-0-0	0-0-0-0	0-0-0-0	0-0-0-0	0-0-0-0
String:	1-4-4-1	1-4-4-1	2-5-5-2	2-5-5-2	3-6-6-3	3-6-6-3

27

	⊓ V ⊓ V	⊓ V ⊓ V	⊓ V ⊓ V
Fret:	0-0-0-0	0-0-0-0	0-0-0-0
String:	1-4-4-1	2-5-5-2	3-6-6-3

28

	⊓ V ⊓ V	⊓ V ⊓ V	⊓ V ⊓ V	⊓ V ⊓ V
Fret:	0-0-0-0	0-0-0-0	0-0-0-0	0-0-0-0
String:	5-1-1-5	5-1-1-5	6-2-2-6	6-2-2-6

29

	⊓ V ⊓ V	⊓ V ⊓ V
Fret:	0-0-0-0	0-0-0-0
String:	5-1-1-5	6-2-2-6

30

	⊓ V ⊓ V	⊓ V ⊓ V	⊓ V ⊓ V	⊓ V ⊓ V
Fret:	0-0-0-0	0-0-0-0	0-0-0-0	0-0-0-0
String:	1-5-5-1	1-5-5-1	2-6-6-2	2-6-6-2

31

	⊓ V ⊓ V	⊓ V ⊓ V
Fret:	0-0-0-0	0-0-0-0
String:	1-5-5-1	2-6-6-2

32

	⊓ V ⊓ V	⊓ V ⊓ V
Fret:	0-0-0-0	0-0-0-0
String:	6-1-1-6	6-1-1-6

33

	⊓ V ⊓ V	⊓ V ⊓ V
Fret:	0-0-0-0	0-0-0-0
String:	1-6-6-1	1-6-6-1

To create more exercises for further technical development, combine the exercises presented for the left hand with exercises for the right hand. A couple of sample exercises are shown below.

	⊓ V ⊓ V	⊓ V ⊓ V	⊓ V ⊓ V	⊓ V ⊓ V	⊓ V ⊓ V
Fret:	2-3-4-1	2-3-4-1	2-3-4-1	2-3-4-1	2-3-4-1
String:	1-2-1-2	2-3-2-3	3-4-3-4	4-5-4-5	5-6-5-6

	⊓ V ⊓ V	⊓ V ⊓ V	⊓ V ⊓ V	⊓ V ⊓ V
Fret:	3-1-2-4	3-1-2-4	3-1-2-4	3-1-2-4
String:	3-1 3-1	4-2-4-2	5-3-5-3	6-4-6-4

	⊓ V ⊓ V	⊓ V ⊓ V	⊓ V ⊓ V	⊓ V ⊓ V	⊓ V ⊓ V
Fret:	1-2-3-4	1-2-3-4	1-2-3-4	1-2-3-4	1-2-3-4
String:	2-1-1-2	3-2-2-3	4-3-3-4	5-4-4-5	6-5-5-6

	⊓ V ⊓ V	⊓ V ⊓ V	⊓ V ⊓ V	⊓ V ⊓ V
Fret:	1-4-2-3	1-4-2-3	1-4-2-3	1-4-2-3
String:	1-3-3-1	2-4-4-2	3-5-5-3	4-6-6-4

	⊓ V ⊓ V	⊓ V ⊓ V	⊓ V ⊓ V	⊓ V ⊓ V	⊓ V ⊓ V
Fret:	1-3-2-4	1-3-2-4	1-3-2-4	1-3-2-4	1-3-2-4
String:	1-2-2-1	2-3-3-2	3-4-4-3	5-4-5-4	6-5-5-6

* Remember: the fret number is the left-hand finger number if the patterns are moved out of first position. All of the patterns for the left hand are moveable.

By combining every left-hand four-fingered combination (permutation) with every possible four-string combination, an enormous number of technique-building exercises can be formulated. Many of the string sets are found below. Each of these base sets may be permutated to create twenty-four original sets. These string sets may then be combined with any of the left-hand fingerings that were presented earlier in the book. It doesn't take long to figure out that there are a lot of combinations possible.

Possible String Sets

Strings:	1234	1235	1236	1246	1256	1345
Strings:	1346	1456	2345	2356	2456	3456

The process for deriving all the respective sets is outlined below.

1	2	3	4	Order of original set
1234	2134	3124	4123	Set 1234 yields the following string groups
1243	2143	3142	4132	Last two digits are reversed
1324	2314	3214	4213	Second number is next highest–last two digits in order
1342	2341	3241	4231	Last two digits are reversed
1423	2413	3412	4312	Second number is next highest–last two digits in order
1432	2431	3421	4321	Last two digits are reversed

String Set 2-3-4-5

2345	3245	4235	5234
2354	3254	4253	5243
2435	3425	4325	5324
2453	3452	4352	5342
2534	3524	4523	5423
2543	3542	4532	5432

An example of how to combine a string grouping and a left-hand fingering is shown below.

Fret: 1-3-2-4	(Move this pattern like the other patterns after its completion.
String: 2-4-3-5	Reverse the direction when the fourth finger reaches the 12th fret.)

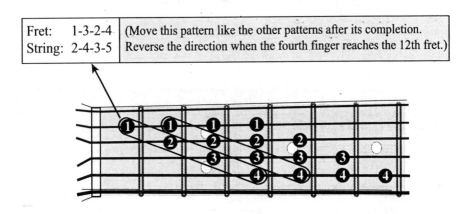

Each guitarist can figure out the rest of the combinations (there are a lot of combinations!). Mix the plethora of possible string groupings with the many left-hand fingering combinations. Then move each exercise up one fret after its completion as discussed previously. These exercises will facilitate "Killer Technique."

All the previous examples for the left-hand have worked the fingers while in a fixed position. Moving the patterns up or down one fret each time the pattern is completed is a good start at getting the left hand moving in a horizontal fashion, but doesn't really facilitate good linear motion. The following exercises should be repeated on all six strings even though they are only shown on one string. They will help all guitarists become more accurate when moving up and down the neck of the guitar.

First, select any note on the first string between frets five and ten. Then, play that same one note with each of the four left-hand fingers. Play this exercises slowly at first. This is a good way to develop accuracy when the left hand has to move up and down the neck.

Fret	**7-7-7-7**
Fingering	**1-2-3-4-etc.**
String	**1-1-1-1**

Here's another good linear movement workout. Notice the notes played on the guitar move down and up the neck while the left-hand fingering moves in the opposite direction. Remember to play these exercises on all six strings.

Fret	**7-6-5-4-5-6-7**
Fingering	**1-2-3-4-3-2-1**
String	**1-1-1-1-1-1-1**

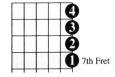

Notice the notes played on the guitar move down and up the neck while the left-hand fingering moves in the opposite direction. Play this exercise on all six strings.

Each of the four left-hand fingered patterns can also be moved up and down the neck on one string. Make sure to play through the position shift seamlessly without skipping a beat or even pausing. Also be sure to reverse the direction of the left-hand movement.

Fret	1-3-2-4-5-7-6-8-9-11-10-12
Fingering	1-3-2-4-1-3-2-4-1 - 3 - 2 - 4
String	1-1-1-1-1-1-1-1-1 - 1 - 1 - 1

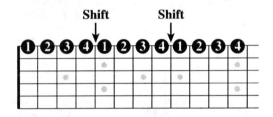

Have fun with all of these exercises.

Corey